Animals Growing Up™

I0889132

How Wolves Grow Up

Linda Bozzo

Enslow Publishing
101 W. 23rd Street
Suite 240
New York, NY 10011
USA

enslow.com

WORDS TO KNOW

carnivores Animals that eat meat.

den The home of a wild animal, such as a wolf.

litter A group of young animals born at the same time to one mother.

mammals Warm-blooded animals that breathe air, have backbones and hair, and produce milk for their young.

packs Groups of animals that live and hunt together.

predators Animals that kill and eat other animals to live.

prey An animal that is killed and eaten by another animal.

pups Baby wolves.

social skills Behaviors that help the pack work together.

territory A pack's home area.

CONTENTS

WORDS TO KNOW 2

WOLF PACKS 4

COZY DENS 6

LITTERMATES 8

A SAFE HOME 10

A PUP'S DIET 12

MEETINGS 14

PLAYTIME 16

DINNER 18

PUPS HUNTING 20

LEAVING HOME 22

LEARN MORE. 24

INDEX. 24

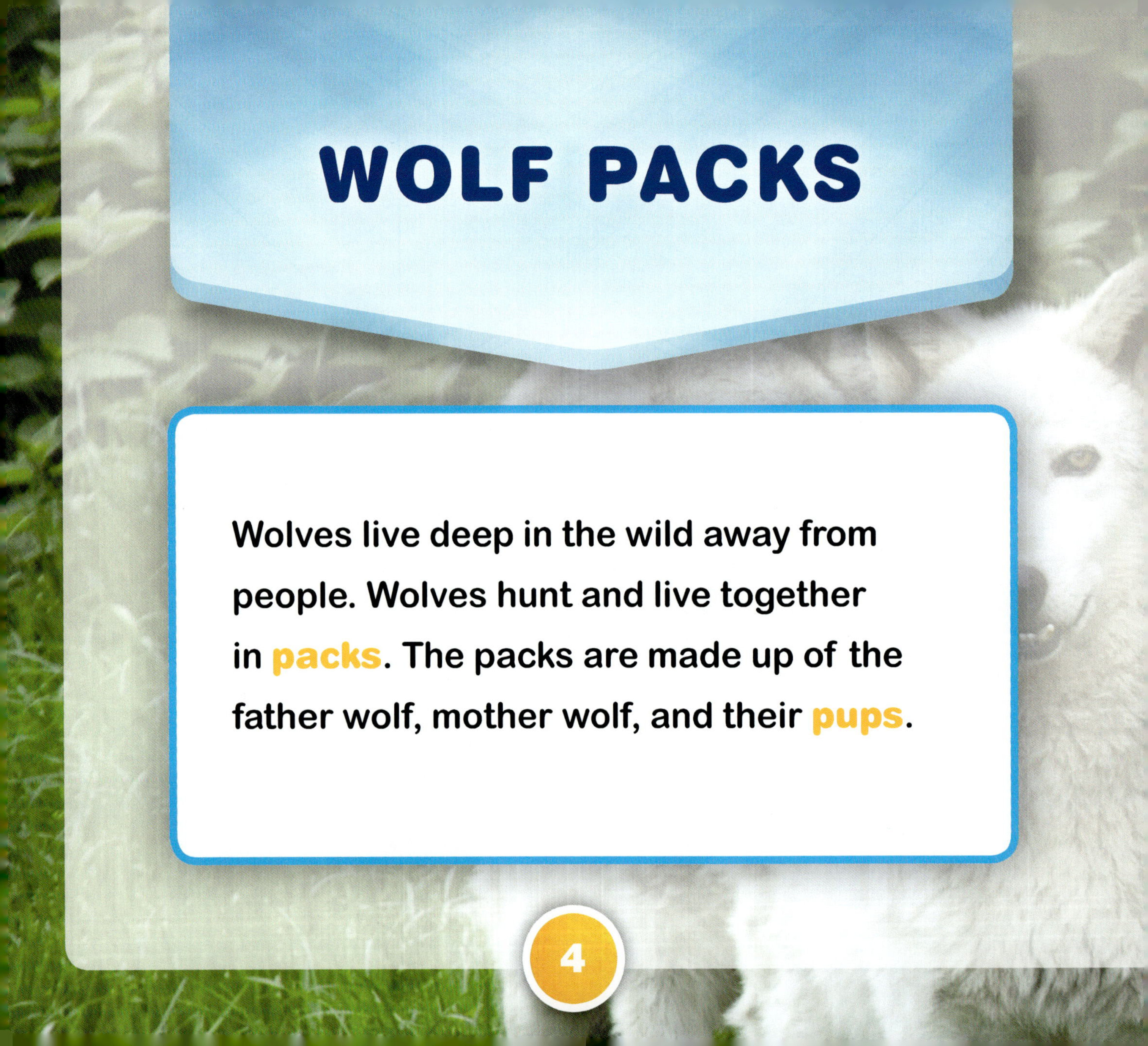

WOLF PACKS

Wolves live deep in the wild away from people. Wolves hunt and live together in **packs**. The packs are made up of the father wolf, mother wolf, and their **pups**.

FAST FACT

Wolves are closely related to dogs.

A pack of European gray wolves hunts together.

COZY DENS

A mother wolf carries her babies inside her for about 63 days. Then the wolf pups are born in the parent wolves' **den**. This could be a small cave or a hole dug in the ground.

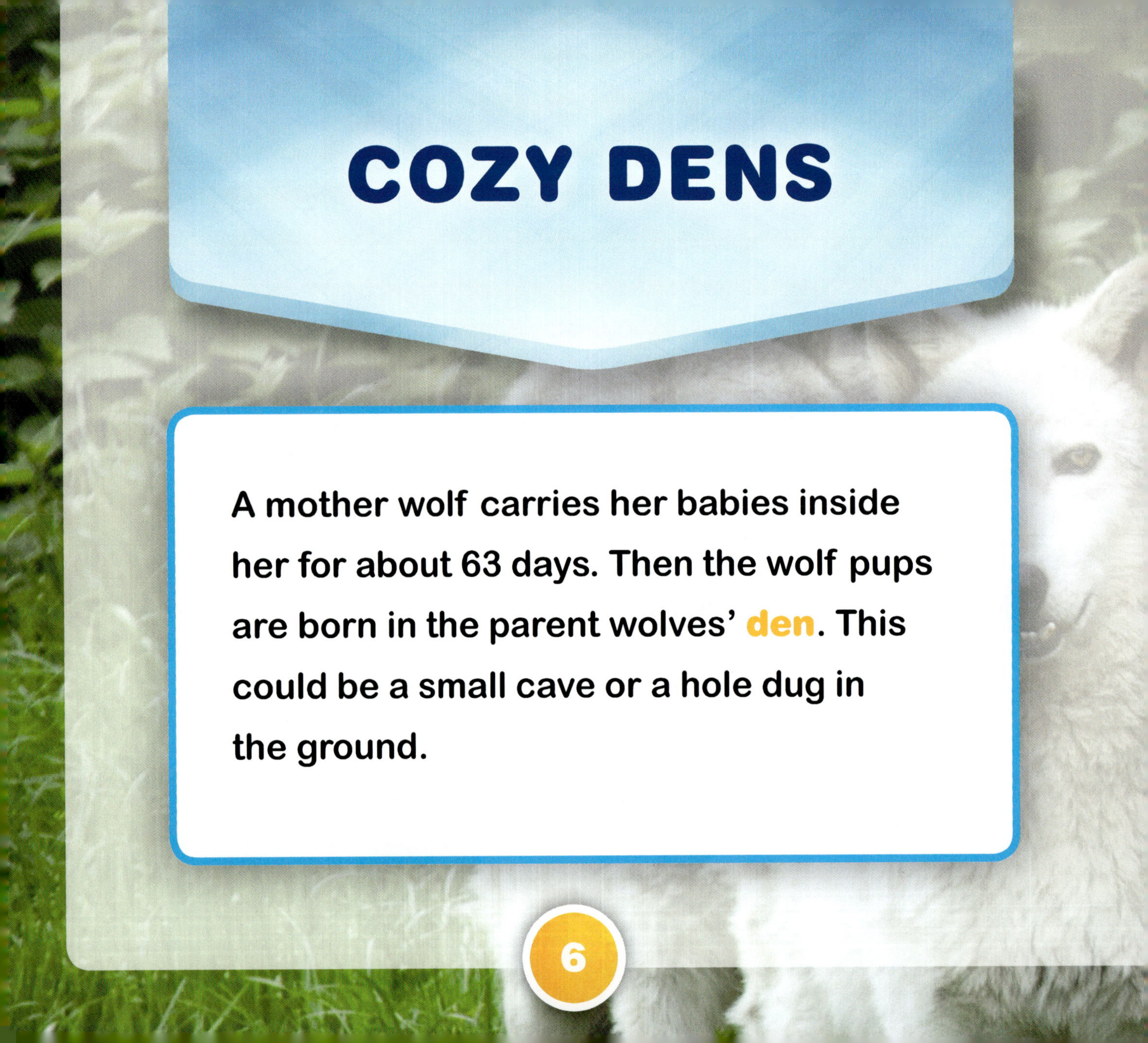

A mother wolf watches over her pups in the family den.

FAST FACT

Some packs use the same den for years. Others might use a new den every year.

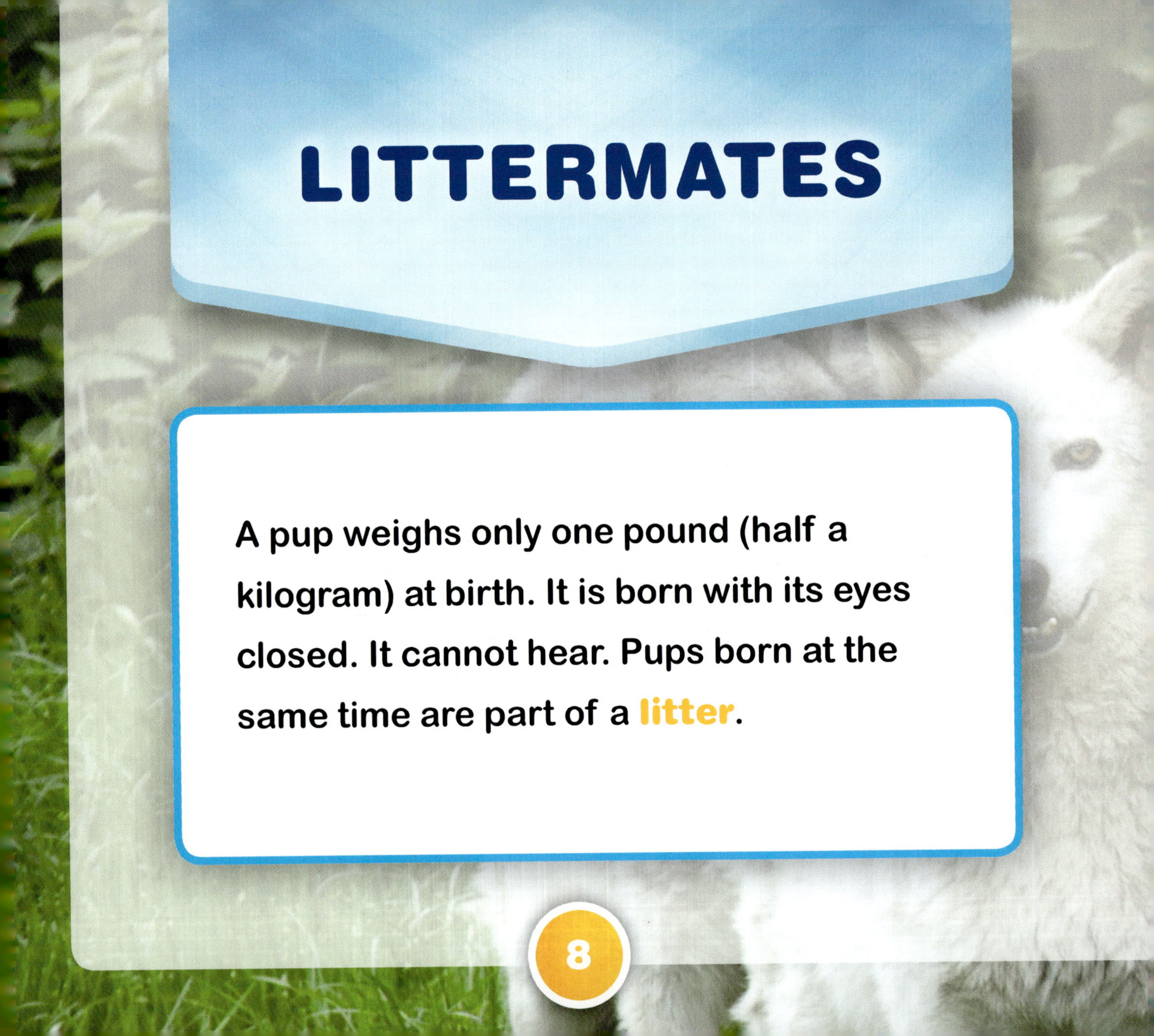

LITTERMATES

A pup weighs only one pound (half a kilogram) at birth. It is born with its eyes closed. It cannot hear. Pups born at the same time are part of a **litter**.

FAST FACT

A mother wolf gives birth to about four to six pups in a litter.

The pups' eyes begin to open at about two weeks old. Their eyes are blue.

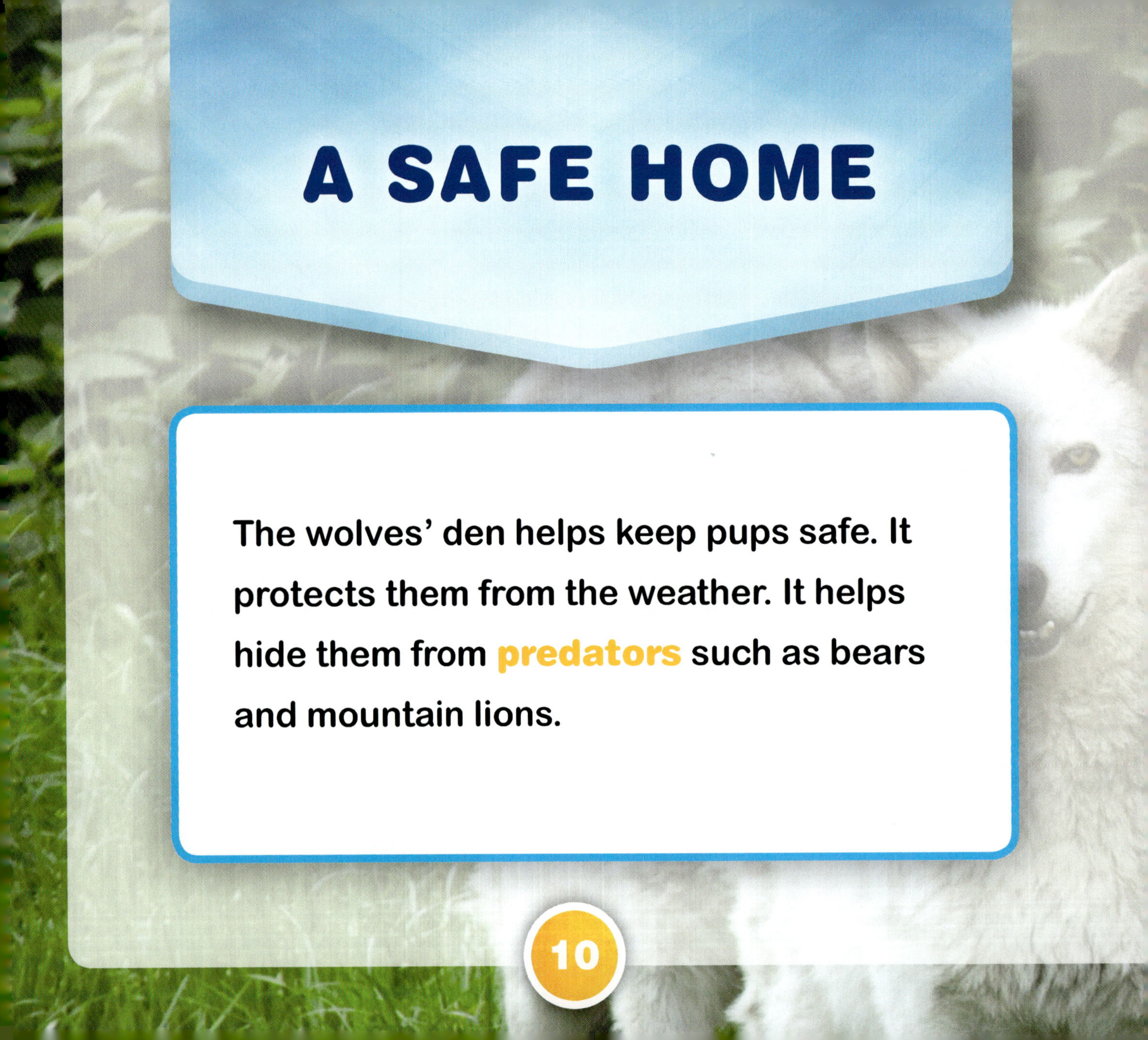

A SAFE HOME

The wolves' den helps keep pups safe. It protects them from the weather. It helps hide them from **predators** such as bears and mountain lions.

FAST FACT

After about three weeks, pups will start to explore the den.

A gray wolf pup pokes its head out of the den. It is ready to explore!

A PUP'S DIET

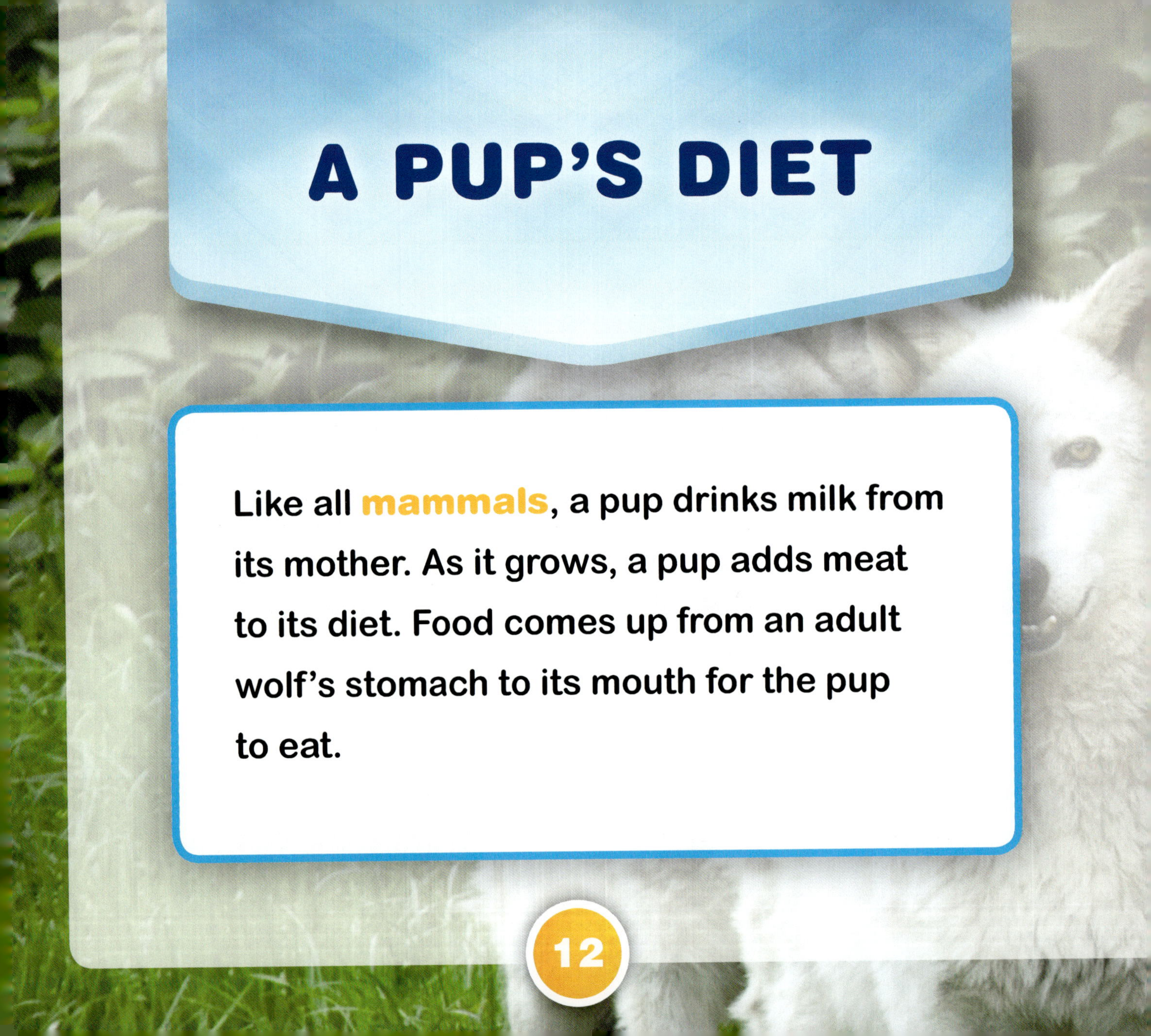

Like all **mammals**, a pup drinks milk from its mother. As it grows, a pup adds meat to its diet. Food comes up from an adult wolf's stomach to its mouth for the pup to eat.

FAST FACT

All female adult wolves in the pack produce milk for the pups.

A litter of pups drinks milk from the mother wolf.

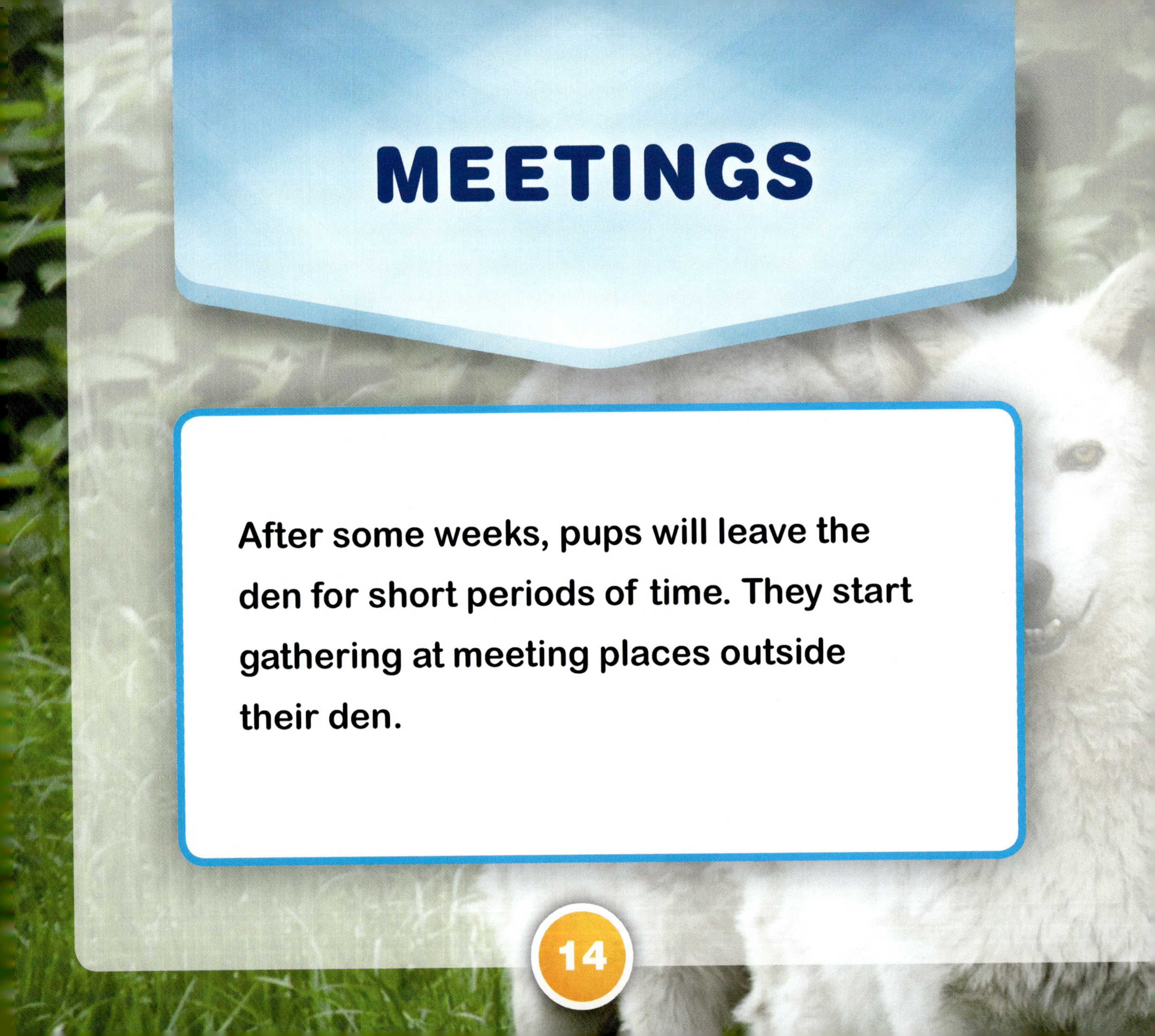

MEETINGS

After some weeks, pups will leave the den for short periods of time. They start gathering at meeting places outside their den.

FAST FACT

Pups sleep and play at these meeting places until they are old enough to hunt with their pack.

Three pups leave their den to gather at the meeting place.

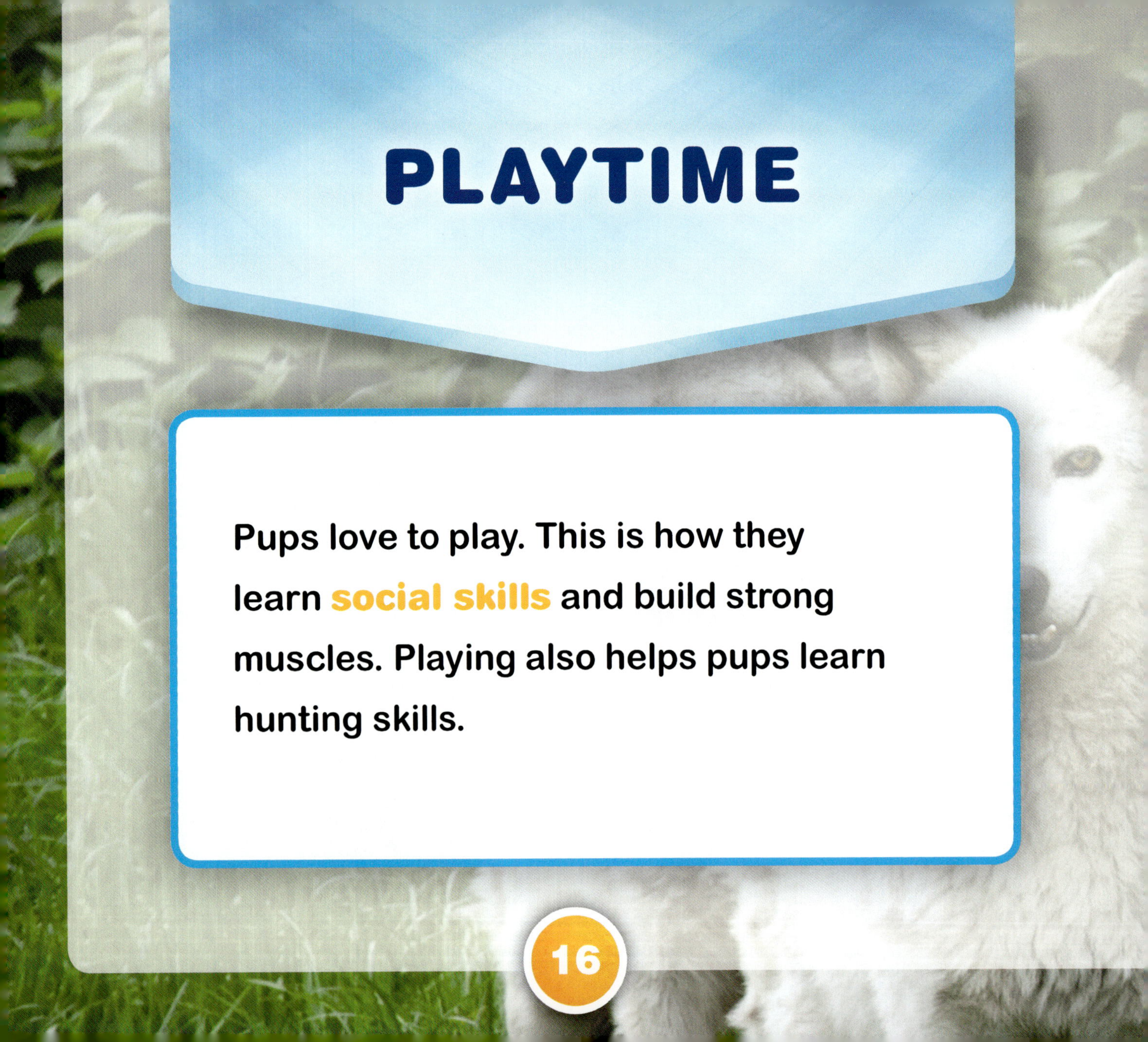

PLAYTIME

Pups love to play. This is how they learn **social skills** and build strong muscles. Playing also helps pups learn hunting skills.

FAST FACT

Wolves have powerful jaws that can break the bones of other animals.

A playful pup pounces on its littermate. These pups are practicing hunting skills they will need as adults.

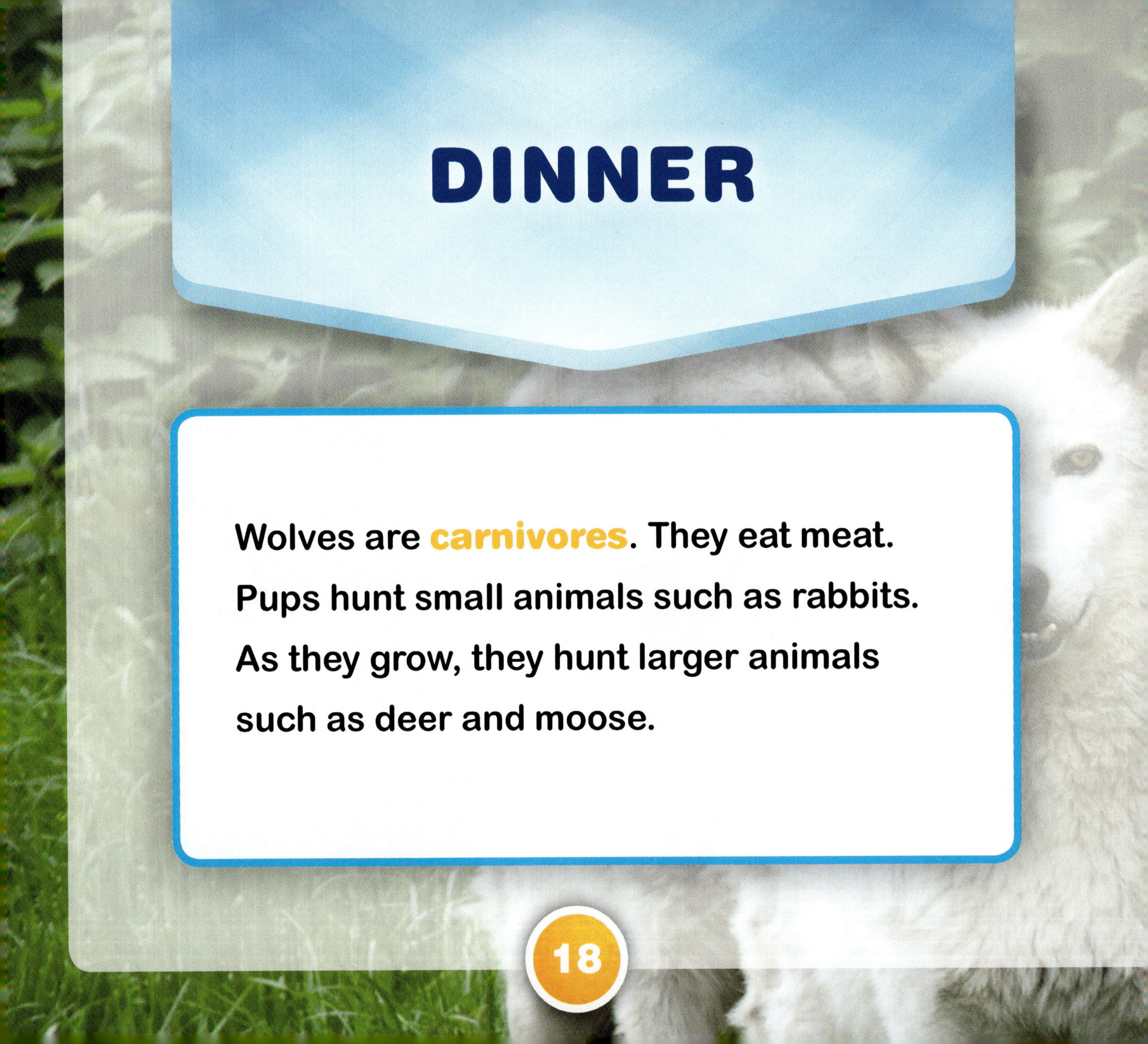

DINNER

Wolves are **carnivores**. They eat meat. Pups hunt small animals such as rabbits. As they grow, they hunt larger animals such as deer and moose.

A pup takes a meaty bone from an animal its pack has killed.

FAST FACT

Wolves have very large stomachs for their very large meals!

PUPS HUNTING

Pups soon join their pack on hunts. A pup's job is to tire out the **prey** by chasing it around. An adult wolf makes the kill.

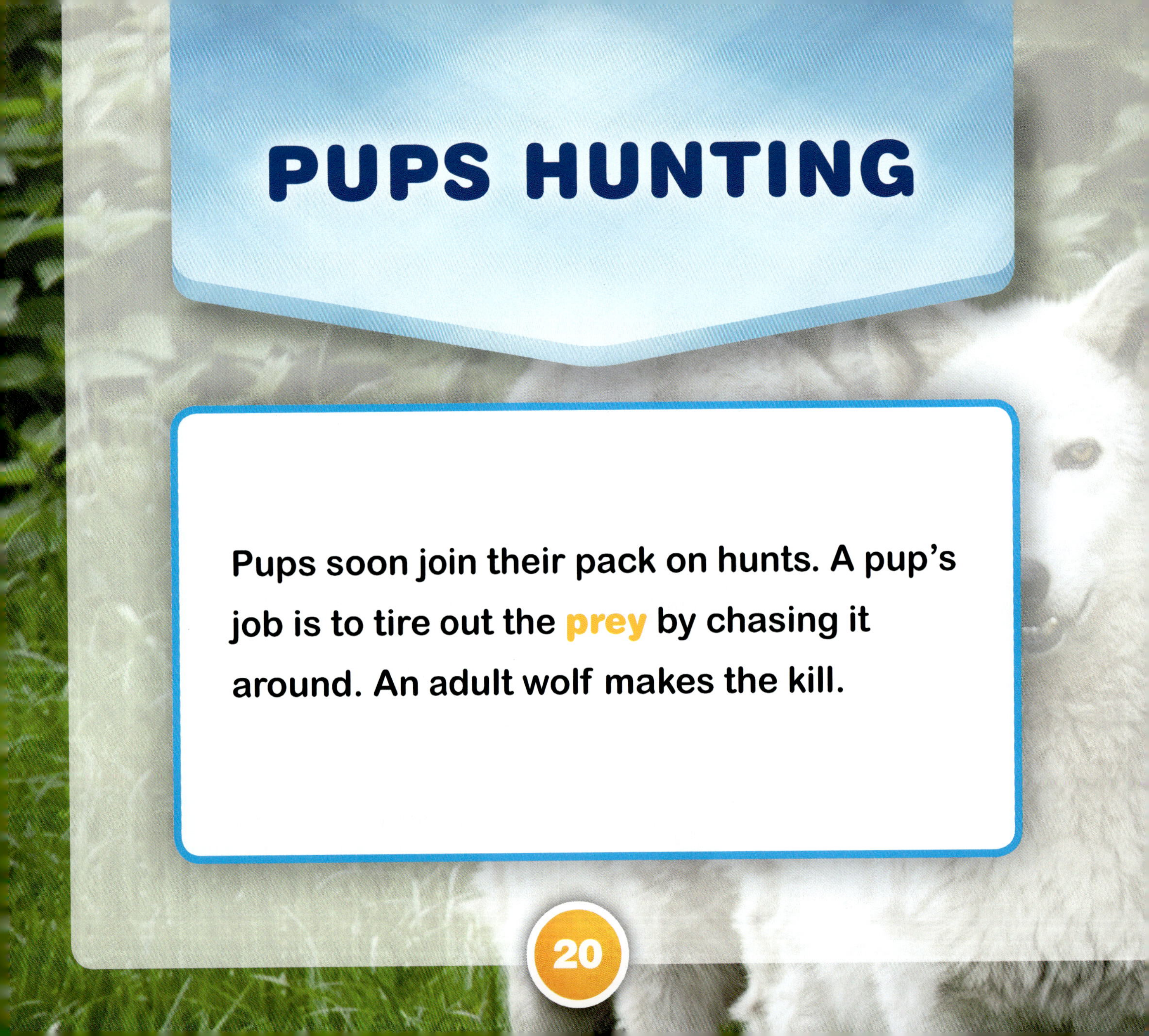

FAST FACT

Each wolf pack has its own howl.

An Arctic wolf pup practices its howl.

LEAVING HOME

At two or three years old, the pups will leave home. They will look for **territory** away from other wolves. They are ready to start packs of their own.

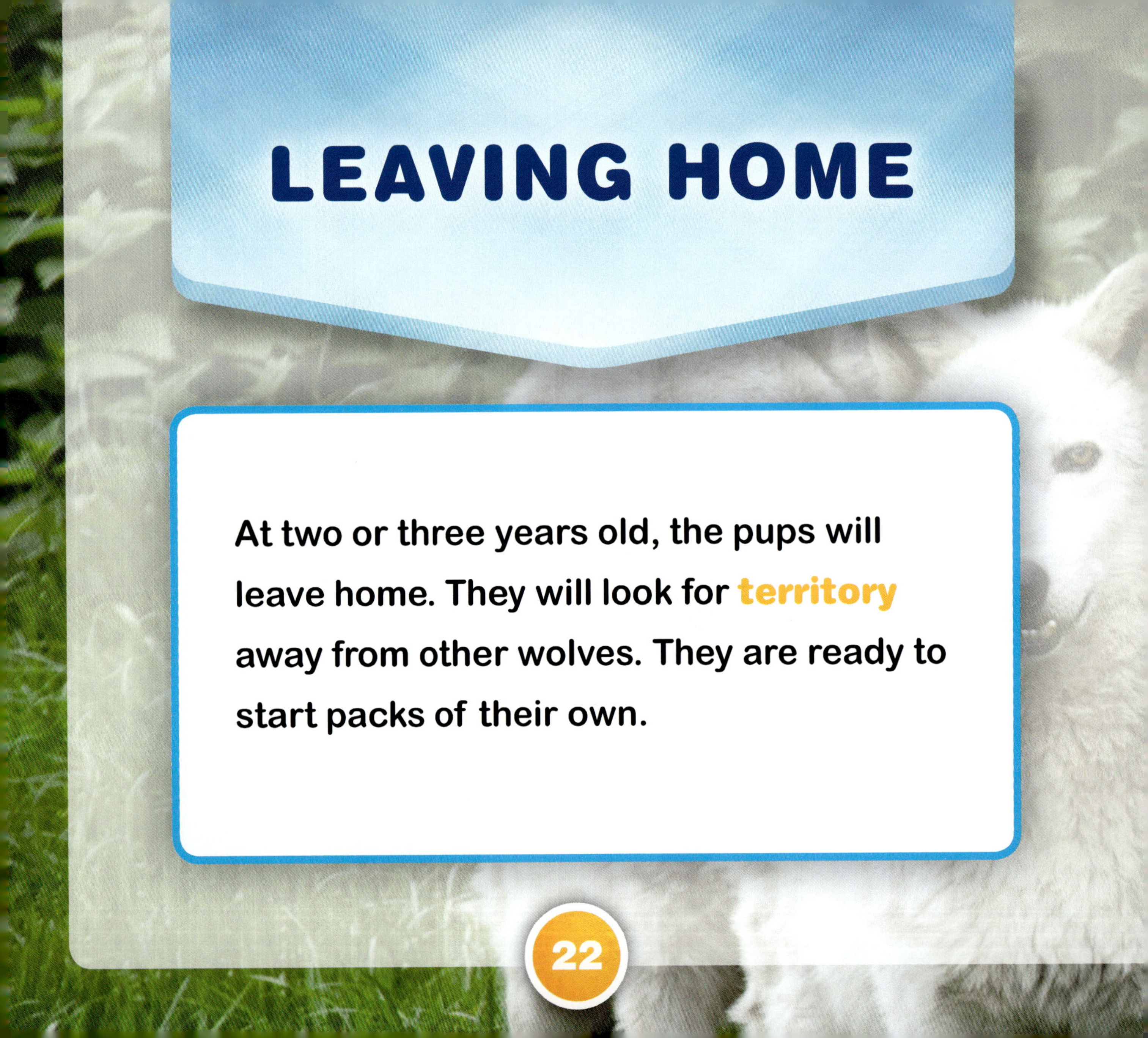

Three young wolves patrol their territory.

FAST FACT

Wolves live about six to eight years in the wild.

LEARN MORE

Books

American Museum of Natural History. *Wolf Pups Join the Pack.* New York, NY: Sterling Children's Books, 2017.

Brannon, Cecelia. *Baby Wolves at the Zoo.* New York, NY: Enslow Publishing, 2016.

Kelley, K. C. *Baby Wolves.* Mankato, MN: Amicus Ink, 2018.

Websites

International Wolf Center
wolf.org/wolf-info/wild-kids/wild-kids-articles
Read fun facts and stories about wolves.

National Geographic Kids: Gray Wolf
kids.nationalgeographic.com/animals/gray-wolf
Get a close-up look at the gray wolf.

INDEX

birth, 6, 8, 9
carnivores, 18
den, 6, 7, 10, 11, 14
dogs, 5
eyes, 8
hearing, 8
howl, 21
hunting, 4, 15, 16, 18, 20
jaws, 17
leaving home, 22
life span, 23
litter, 8, 9
mammals, 12
meat, 12, 18
meeting places, 14, 15
milk, 12, 13
packs, 4, 7, 13, 15, 20, 21, 22
playing, 15, 16
predators, 10
prey, 20
sleeping, 15
social skills, 16
stomach, 12, 19
territory, 22

Published in 2020 by Enslow Publishing, LLC.
101 W. 23rd Street, Suite 240, New York, NY 10011

Library of Congress Cataloging-in-Publication Data

Names: Bozzo, Linda, author.
Title: How wolves grow up / Linda Bozzo.
Description: New York : Enslow Publishing, 2020. | Series: Animals growing up | Audience: K to Grade 3. | Includes bibliographical references and index.
Identifiers: LCCN 2018049546| ISBN 9781978507241 (library bound) | ISBN 9781978508347 (paperback) | ISBN 9781978508354 (6 pack)
Subjects: LCSH: Wolves—Development—Juvenile literature. | Wolves—Infancy—Juvenile literature.
Classification: LCC QL737.C22 B628 2020 | DDC 599.77313/92—dc23
LC record available at https://lccn.loc.gov/2018049546

Printed in the United States of America

Photo Credits: Cover, p. 1 Debbie Steinhausser/Shutterstock.com; interior pages 4–23 (background), 5 (main photo) Alan Jeffery/Shutterstock.com; p. 7 Daniel J. Cox/Oxford Scientific/Getty Images; p. 9 Tom Walker/Visuals Unlimited/Getty Images; pp. 11, 17 Holly Kuchera/Shutterstock.com; p. 13 Jim Cumming/Moment/Getty Images; p. 15 A.von Dueren/Shutterstock.com; p. 19 Frenchwildlifephotograher/Shutterstock.com; p. 21 critterbiz/Shutterstock.com; p. 23 David Dirga/Shutterstock.com; back cover and additional interior pages background graphic 13Imagery/Shutterstock.com.